Jazz Piano Solos Volume 35
stride piano

Arranged by Brent Edstrom

contents

- 2   AIN'T MISBEHAVIN'
- 6   CAROLINA SHOUT
- 13 DINAH
- 18 FINGERBUSTER
- 26 HANDFUL OF KEYS
- 31 HONEYSUCKLE ROSE
- 36 IT'S THE TALK OF THE TOWN
- 39 JITTERBUG WALTZ
- 44 LIZA
- 49 LULU'S BACK IN TOWN
- 54 MAKIN' WHOOPEE!
- 58 MEMORIES OF YOU
- 63 NUMB FUMBLIN'
- 68 ROSETTA
- 72 SMASHING THIRDS
- 78 SQUEEZE ME
- 81 TEA FOR TWO
- 86 VIPER'S DRAG
- 92 WILLOW WEEP FOR ME

ISBN 978-1-4950-0751-4

HAL•LEONARD® CORPORATION
7777 W. BLUEMOUND RD. P.O. BOX 13819 MILWAUKEE, WI 53213

For all works contained herein:
Unauthorized copying, arranging, adapting, recording, Internet posting, public performance,
or other distribution of the printed music in this publication is an infringement of copyright.
Infringers are liable under the law.

Visit Hal Leonard Online at
www.halleonard.com

AIN'T MISBEHAVIN'

Words by ANDY RAZAF
Music by THOMAS "FATS" WALLER
and HARRY BROOKS

CAROLINA SHOUT

By JAMES P. JOHNSON

Moderate Stride

R.H. 8va until 2nd ending

Arrangement based on one by James P. Johnson

Copyright © 1925 UNIVERSAL MUSIC CORP.
Copyright Renewed
This arrangement Copyright © 2015 UNIVERSAL MUSIC CORP.
All Rights Reserved   Used by Permission

DINAH
from THE BIG BROADCAST

Words by SAM M. LEWIS and JOE YOUNG
Music by HARRY AKST

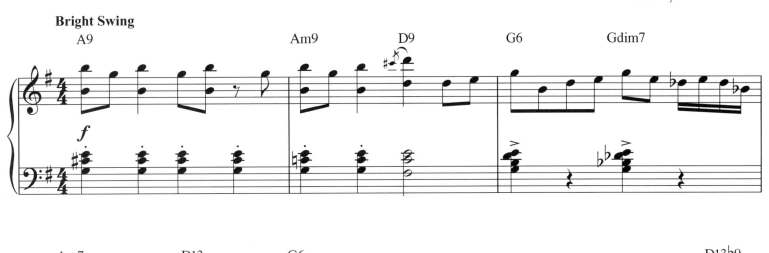
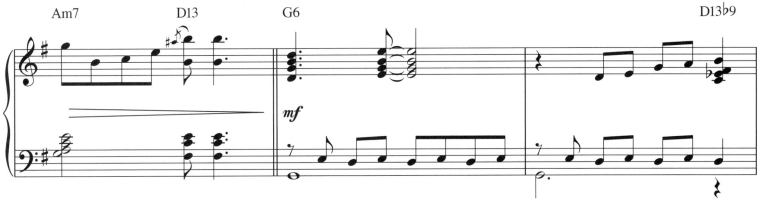

FINGERBUSTER
(Fingerbreaker)

Words and Music by
FERD "JELLY ROLL" MORTON

Arrangement based on one by Ferd "Jelly Roll" Morton and Dick Hyman

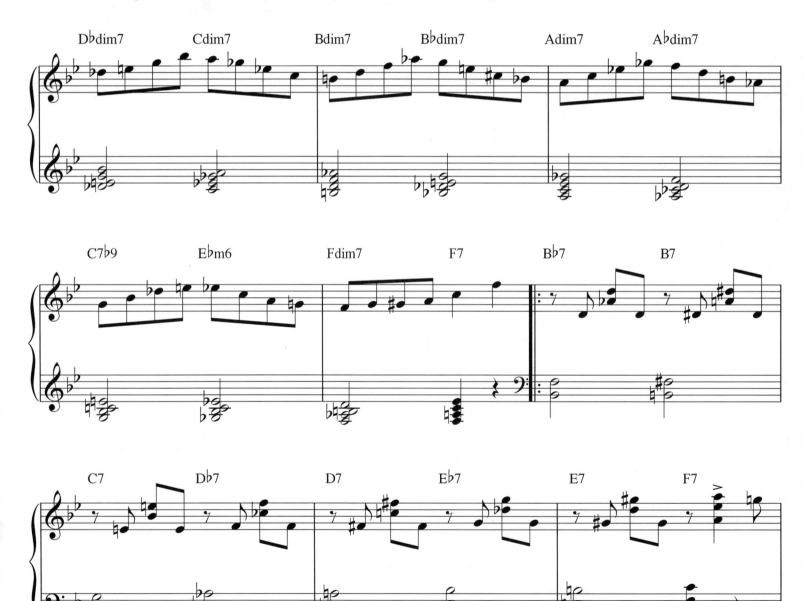

Copyright © 1938 Roy J. Carew Co.
Copyright Renewed
This arrangement Copyright © 2015 Roy J. Carew Co.
All Rights Renewed   Used by Permission

HANDFUL OF KEYS
from AIN'T MISBEHAVIN'

Music by THOMAS "FATS" WALLER

Arrangement based on one by Fats Waller

© 1930 (Renewed) CHAPPELL & CO., INC.
This arrangement © 2015 CHAPPELL & CO., INC.
All Rights Reserved   Used by Permission

HONEYSUCKLE ROSE
from AIN'T MISBEHAVIN'

Words by ANDY RAZAF
Music by THOMAS "FATS" WALLER

IT'S THE TALK OF THE TOWN

Words by MARTY SYMES and AL NEIBURG
Music by JERRY LIVINGSTON

JITTERBUG WALTZ

Music by
THOMAS "FATS" WALLER

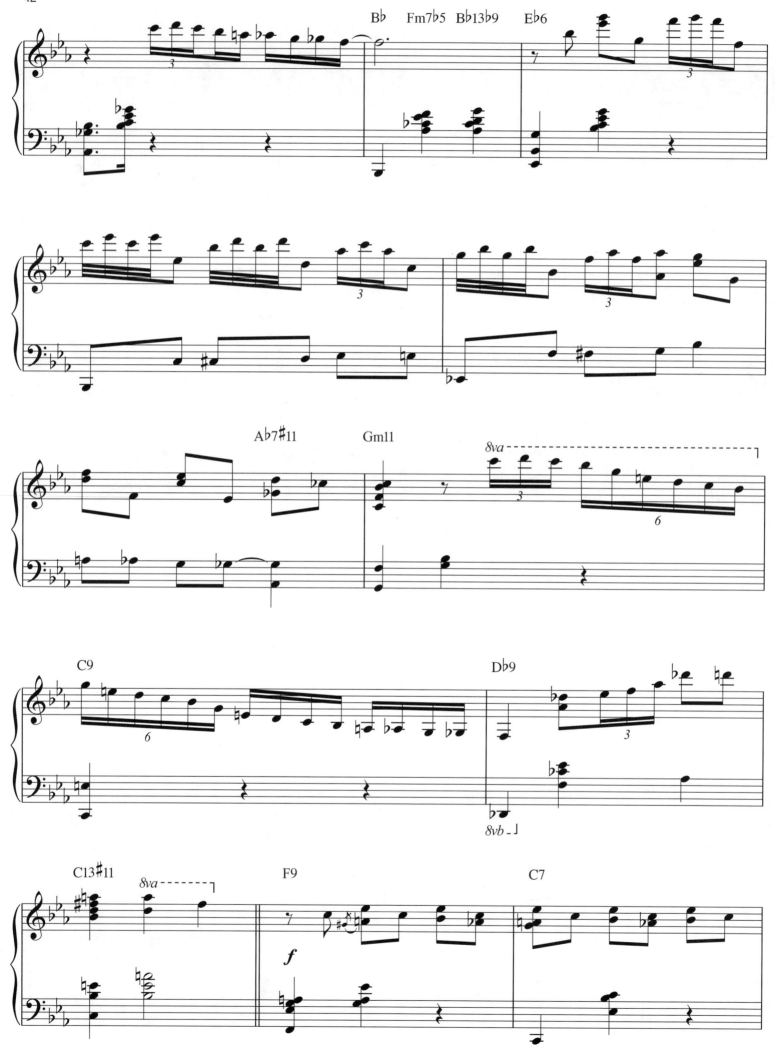

LIZA
(All the Clouds'll Roll Away)

Music by GEORGE GERSHWIN
Lyrics by IRA GERSHWIN and GUS KAHN

LULU'S BACK IN TOWN

Words by AL DUBIN
Music by HARRY WARREN

© 1935 (Renewed) WB MUSIC CORP.
This arrangement © 2015 WB MUSIC CORP.
All Rights Reserved   Used by Permission

54

MAKIN' WHOOPEE!
from WHOOPEE!

Lyrics by GUS KAHN
Music by WALTER DONALDSON

Copyright © 1928 (Renewed) by Donaldson Publishing Co., Dreyer Music Co. and Gilbert Keyes Music Company
This arrangement Copyright © 2015 by Donaldson Publishing Co., Dreyer Music Co. and Gilbert Keyes Music Company
All Rights for Dreyer Music Co. Administered by Larry Spier, Inc., New York
All Rights for Gilbert Keyes Music Company Administered by WB Music Corp.
International Copyright Secured All Rights Reserved

MEMORIES OF YOU
from THE BENNY GOODMAN STORY

Lyric by ANDY RAZAF
Music by EUBIE BLAKE

NUMB FUMBLIN'

By THOMAS "FATS" WALLER

ROSETTA

Words and Music by EARL HINES
and HENRI WOOD

SQUEEZE ME

Words and Music by CLARENCE WILLIAMS
and THOMAS "FATS" WALLER

Arrangement based on one by James P. Johnson

Copyright © 1925 UNIVERSAL MUSIC CORP. and GREAT STANDARDS MUSIC PUBLISHING COMPANY
Copyright Renewed
This arrangement Copyright © 2015 UNIVERSAL MUSIC CORP. and GREAT STANDARDS MUSIC PUBLISHING COMPANY
All Rights for GREAT STANDARDS MUSIC PUBLISHING COMPANY Controlled and Administered by THE SONGWRITERS GUILD OF AMERICA
All Rights Reserved   Used by Permission

TEA FOR TWO
from NO, NO, NANETTE

Words by IRVING CAESAR
Music by VINCENT YOUMANS

VIPER'S DRAG

By THOMAS "FATS" WALLER

Moderate Swing

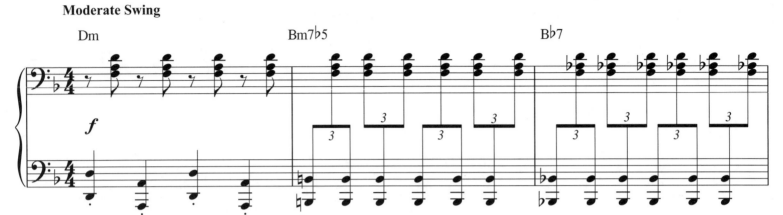

Arrangement based on one by Thomas "Fats" Waller

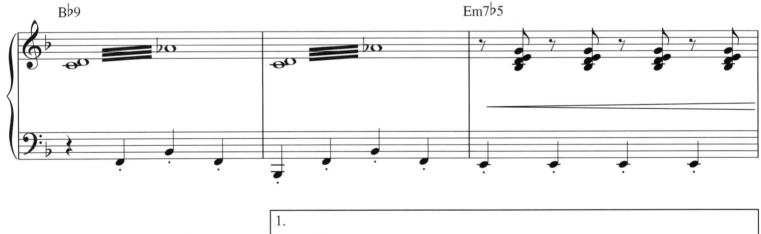

© 1930, 1934 (Renewed) EDWIN H. MORRIS & COMPANY, A Division of MPL Music Publishing, Inc. and CHAPPELL & CO.
This arrangement © 2015 EDWIN H. MORRIS & COMPANY, A Division of MPL Music Publishing, Inc. and CHAPPELL & CO.
All Rights Reserved

WILLOW WEEP FOR ME

Words and Music by
ANN RONELL

Arrangement based on one by Art Tatum

Copyright © 1932 by Bourne Co. (ASCAP)
Copyright Renewed by Ann Ronell Music
This arrangement Copyright © 2015 Ann Ronell Music
All Rights in the U.S. Administered by The Songwriters Guild of America
All Rights outside the U.S. Administered by Bourne Co.
International Copyright Secured   All Rights Reserved

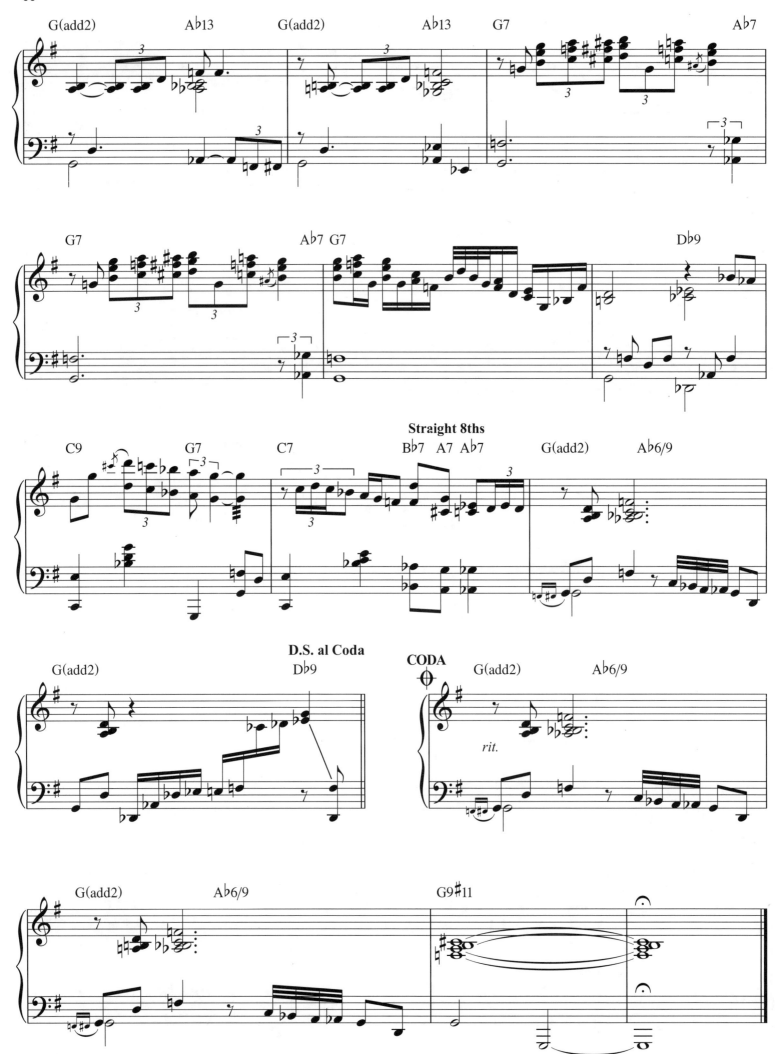